LEARN TO DRAW

This library edition published in 2014 by Walter Foster Publishing,
a Division of the Quayside Publishing Group.
Walter Foster Library
3 Wrigley, Suite A
Irvine, CA 92618

Distributed in the United States and Canada by
Lerner Publisher Services
241 First Avenue North
Minneapolis, MN 55401 U.S.A.
www.lernerbooks.com

First Library Edition

Library of Congress Cataloging-in-Publication Data

Learn to draw Disney Pixar Toy Story : featuring favorite characters from Toy Story 2 & Toy Story 3! /
Illustrated by the Disney Storybook Artists. -- Library edition.
    pages cm
ISBN 978-1-93958-112-9
1. Cartoon characters--Juvenile literature. 2. Drawing--Technique--Juvenile literature. 3. Toy story
(Motion picture)--Juvenile literature. 4. Toy story 2 (Motion picture)--Juvenile literature. 5. Toy story 3
(Motion picture)--Juvenile literature. I. Disney Storybook Artists, illustrator.
 NC1764.L34 2014
 741.5'1--dc23
                                                                                    2013024802

012014
18376

9 8 7 6 5 4 3 2 1

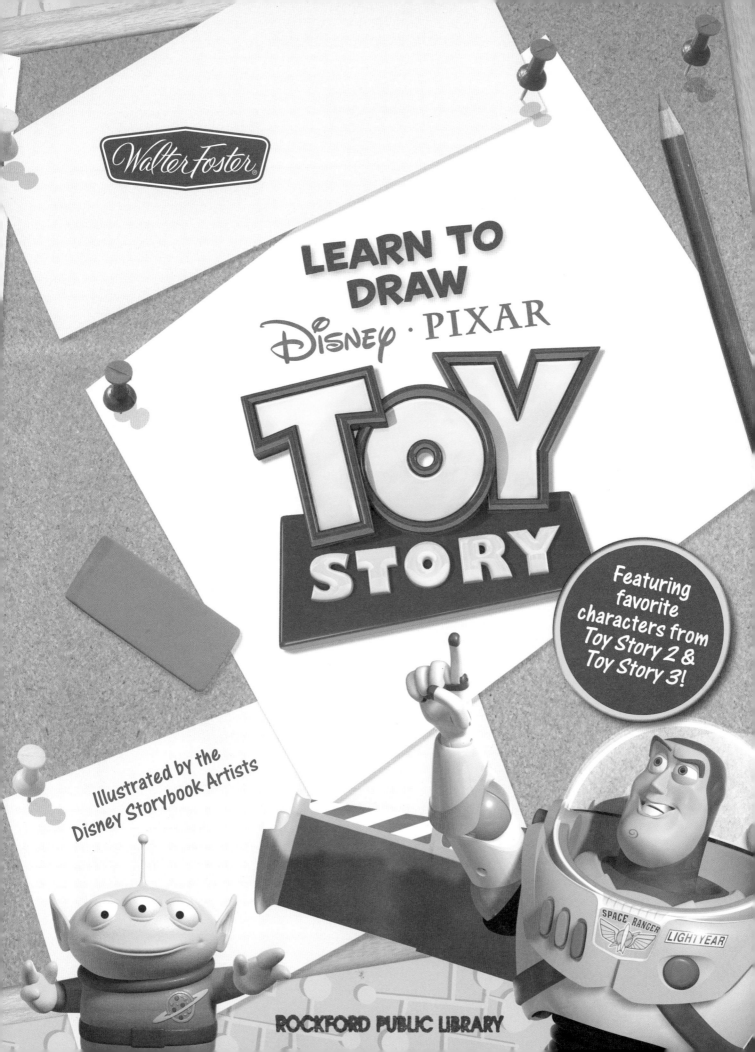

TABLE OF CONTENTS

TOY STORY

As *Toy Story* begins, the toys in Andy's room are nervous. Andy, the young boy who plays with them, is about to have a birthday party. Birthday parties mean presents ... and presents mean new toys. Rex (the toy T. Rex), Slinky Dog, Mr. Potato Head, Hamm (the piggy bank), and the others worry that new toys will take their place. Woody, the cowboy doll who has been Andy's favorite toy for years, tells them not to worry. The most important thing, he reminds them, is that they are all there for Andy.

Woody has to follow his own advice when he sees Andy's newest toy. It is a Buzz Lightyear action figure, with karate-chop motions, laser lights, and pop-out wings. Strangely, Buzz does not realize he is a toy. He believes he is a genuine space ranger, sworn to protect the universe from the evil Emperor Zurg.

Woody tries to keep Buzz from becoming Andy's top toy. But his plan lands both of them in the hands of Sid, the toy-destroying boy next door. Woody and Buzz have to work with each other—and with some very scary mutant toys—to make their way back to Andy. Along the way, they become friends and realize that they are both important to Andy.

TOY STORY 2

In *Toy Story 2*, when Woody tries to help save an older toy from a yard sale, he ends up toy-napped! Al, of Al's Toy Barn, nabs Woody in order to complete his collectible set of toys from *Woody's Roundup,* an old black-and-white TV show.

Al plans to sell the set to a toy museum in Japan. In Al's apartment, Woody meets the rest of his Roundup gang: Bullseye, the sharpest horse in the West; Jessie, the yodeling cowgirl; and the Prospector, the mint-condition miner.

Meanwhile, Buzz and the others from Andy's room race to rescue their pal. After a long adventure, the toys finally arrive at Al's place, where they learn that Woody now *likes* being a collectible! He doesn't want to go back to Andy's room. It turns out the other collectible toys in Al's apartment have convinced him he'll end up in the next yard sale if he doesn't choose to stay with them.

Then it's time for Buzz to step in. He reminds his pal Woody that a toy isn't really a toy until someone plays with it. Woody realizes that Buzz is right. Before any of them can get back to Andy's though, they have to get past some unexpected enemies: The Prospector isn't about to let Woody go; Emperor Zurg is after Buzz; and a new Buzz from Al's toy store threatens Buzz's leader status. Still, the toys from Andy's room manage to rescue Woody, and soon they are giving a "nice, big Andy's room welcome" to Bullseye and Jessie, who are simply rarin' to be played with by their new kid, Andy.

TOY STORY 3

In *Toy Story 3*, Andy is about to leave for college, and Woody and the other toys are worried about what that means for them. When Andy tosses everyone but Woody in a trash bag, the toys are convinced they're being thrown out! Woody insists they're bound for the attic, but when Andy's mom carries them down to the curb, it looks like they're going out with the trash. Woody rushes to

TOY STORY 3

save his friends from the garbage truck, but they manage to escape on their own—and climb into a daycare donation box. Before Woody can convince them to stay, Andy's mom shuts them in the car, and suddenly they're all headed to daycare—even Woody.

At Sunnyside Daycare, Andy's toys see a room full of happy children playing. It's like a dream come true! They meet a crowd of friendly daycare toys, whose leader, Lots-o'-Huggin' Bear—Lotso for short—gives Andy's toys a tour that ends in the Caterpillar

Room, which will be their new home. Woody tries again to convince his friends that they belong with Andy, but they refuse to go back. He leaves alone, but during his escape he gets stuck in a tree. Bonnie, a little girl from daycare, sees Woody and takes him home.

Back in the Caterpillar Room, a horde of shrieking toddlers swarms in. The toys get thrown, kicked, and bitten—it's a nightmare! Buzz catches a glimpse of the Butterfly Room, where the older kids are playing nicely with Lotso and the others. He decides to ask Lotso to help them move into the Butterfly Room.

But he soon discovers that Lotso purposely stuck them in the Caterpillar Room to be destroyed! Before Buzz can warn the others, Lotso's henchman, Big Baby, nabs him! Lotso offers to let Buzz join him in the bigger kids' room, but when Buzz wants to bring his friends too, Lotso turns Buzz to his "demo" mode, which makes Buzz forget who he is.

Buzz's friends start to get worried. Mrs. Potato Head slips one of her eyes under the door to see what's happening, but she sees Andy instead! She figures out that she's seeing out of the eye she left back in Andy's room during the confusion. Andy seems upset as he frantically searches his room. She realizes that he's looking for them! Woody was right—Andy *does* still want them.

Just then, Lotso and his gang enter. Andy's toys rush over to explain that they need to go home. But Lotso tells them they aren't going anywhere. And then a brainwashed Buzz locks them up!

Meanwhile, Woody is enjoying his best playtime in years with Bonnie and her toys, but he's still determined to go home to Andy. When Woody mentions that he came from Sunnyside, Bonnie's toys are shocked that he made it out. They explain that Lotso is a cruel dictator who runs Sunnyside like a prison. Woody realizes he has to go back to save his friends.

Woody sneaks back to Sunnyside in Bonnie's backpack and comes up with a plan to get them all out through the garbage chute. But Lotso and his gang cut them off.

Woody wins over Big Baby, who turns on Lotso and throws the bear in the dumpster. But Lotso pulls Woody into the dumpster, too! Suddenly, the dumpster is emptied into a garbage truck, and all of Andy's toys— and Lotso—tumble in after him.

The toys end up at the dump, riding a conveyer belt toward an incinerator. Lotso sees a "stop" button and climbs up to press it, but at the last minute, he changes his mind and abandons the others. They think they're done for, but then the Aliens scoop them up with "The Clawwww!"—a giant crane!

The toys hitch a ride back to Andy's street on a garbage truck, while Lotso ends up tied to the front grille of another truck.

Back home, Andy is getting ready to leave. Woody climbs into the box marked "College," while the other toys get into a box labeled "Attic." But Woody has an idea and adds his own label to the attic box before climbing into it himself.

Following the note's instructions, Andy takes the box to ... Bonnie's house! Andy introduces each toy to Bonnie, their new owner. He's surprised to see Woody in the donation box, but when he sees how excited Bonnie is to play with Woody, Andy decides to give his favorite cowboy to the little girl too.

The toys watch Andy drive off. They're sad to see him go, but they know they'll always be a part of Andy, and he'll always be a part of them. And they'll always have each other—to infinity and beyond!

TOOLS AND MATERIALS

crayons

eraser

colored pencils

ink pen

paintbrush

Here are some tools you might need to draw and color your favorite *Toy Story* characters: a drawing pencil, an eraser, colored pencils, a pencil sharpener, crayons, felt-tip markers, paint and paintbrushes, and an ink pen. Be sure to have plenty of paper on hand for practice!

drawing
pencil
and paper

paint palette

pencil
sharpener

GETTING STARTED

Just follow these simple steps, and you'll be amazed at how fun and easy drawing can be!

STEP 1
Draw the basic shape of the character; then add simple guidelines to help you place the features.

STEP 2
Each new step is shown in blue. Simply follow the blue lines to add the details.

STEP 3
Erase any lines you don't want to keep.

STEP 4
Use crayons, markers, colored pencils, or paints to add color.

SPACE RANGER   LIGHTYEAR

DRAWING EXERCISES

Warm up your hand by drawing lots of squiggles and shapes.

Draw a circle

Draw a square

Draw an oval

Draw a rectangle

Draw a triangle

If you can draw a few basic shapes, you can draw just about anything!

Circle

Ball

Triangle

Ice cream cone

Pizza

Sun

Square

House

Balloon

Oval

Gift

Submarine

Rectangle

Book

Truck

13

WOODY

Woody is top toy in *Toy Story* and that's a tough spot to share, especially with a new toy named Buzz Lightyear, who thinks he's a *real* space ranger. But in *Toy Story 2,* Woody has learned how to share the limelight with friends, both old and new. In *Toy Story 3*, Woody insists on making his way back to Andy, even though Andy has grown up. But is that really the best future for the toys?

STEP 1

STEP 2

14

round eyes

large iris

ears are flat
on top

STEP 3

YES!

NO!
too
straight

YES!
teeth are one long
rectangle

NO!

15

WOODY

Woody's head and torso are the same height

torso is bean-shaped

Woody's arms and legs are made up of tubular sections that are pinched at the knees and elbows

hat fits
squarely on
head

bandana
accents silhouette

STEP
2

buttons on inside
of sleeve

WOODY

sheriff badge
is a 5-point star

STEP 3

Woody
is about
4 heads
tall

top view of
Woody's hat

there is
stitching
around the
edges

hat band comes up 1/4
of hat height

buckle has a
steer-head
design

8 pointed
spurs

forearms
are longer
than upper
arms

calves are
longer than
thighs

Buzz Lightyear

Buzz has stars in his eyes until Woody pulls him back down to Earth. For most of *Toy Story*, Buzz doesn't understand that he's a toy. But in *Toy Story 2*, he understands so well that he has to remind Woody. In *Toy Story 3*, Buzz is captured by a gang of hostile toys, who switch his setting to "demo." Woody and the others rescue him, but when they try to restore his setting, they accidentally switch his language button to Spanish!

STEP 1

STEP 2

STEP 3

iris is about 1/3 the size of the eye

YES!   NO!

brow should barely touch eye in normal pose; keep brows thick

the chin cleft is 1/2 the distance between lower lip and chin

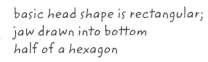

basic head shape is rectangular; jaw drawn into bottom half of a hexagon

Buzz's chin takes up about 1/3 of his head

chin cleft looks like the number 9

eyes can change shape in exaggerated expressions

SPACE RANGER   LIGHTYEAR

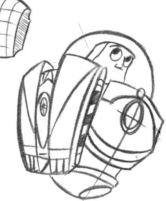

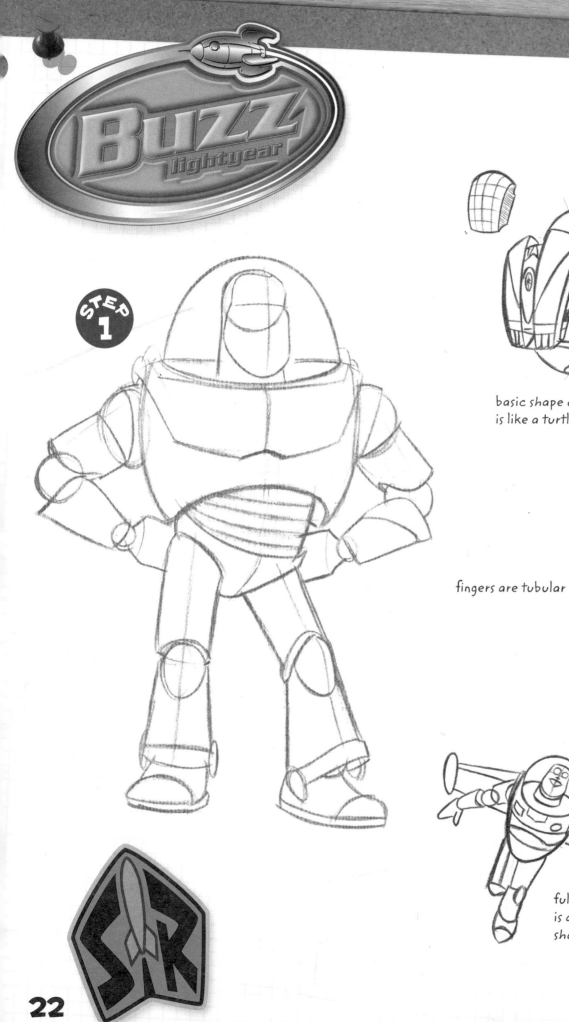

basic shape of backpack
is like a turtle's shell

fingers are tubular

full wingspan
is about 3
shoulder widths

STEP
2

angled

straight

SPACE RANGER LIGHTYEAR

23

arms consist
of cylinders
and spheres

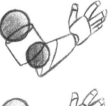

STEP
3

4 grooves on
shoe sole

neck widens into collar

YES!

NO!

legs consist
of 2 sections
connected by
ball joints

SPACE RANGER LIGHTYEAR

LASER

Bullseye, the sharpest horse in the West, is a trusty, energetic steed that loves Woody more than anything else in the world. This proud pony would do almost anything to keep his favorite sheriff out of harm's way.

STEP 1

head is capsule-shaped

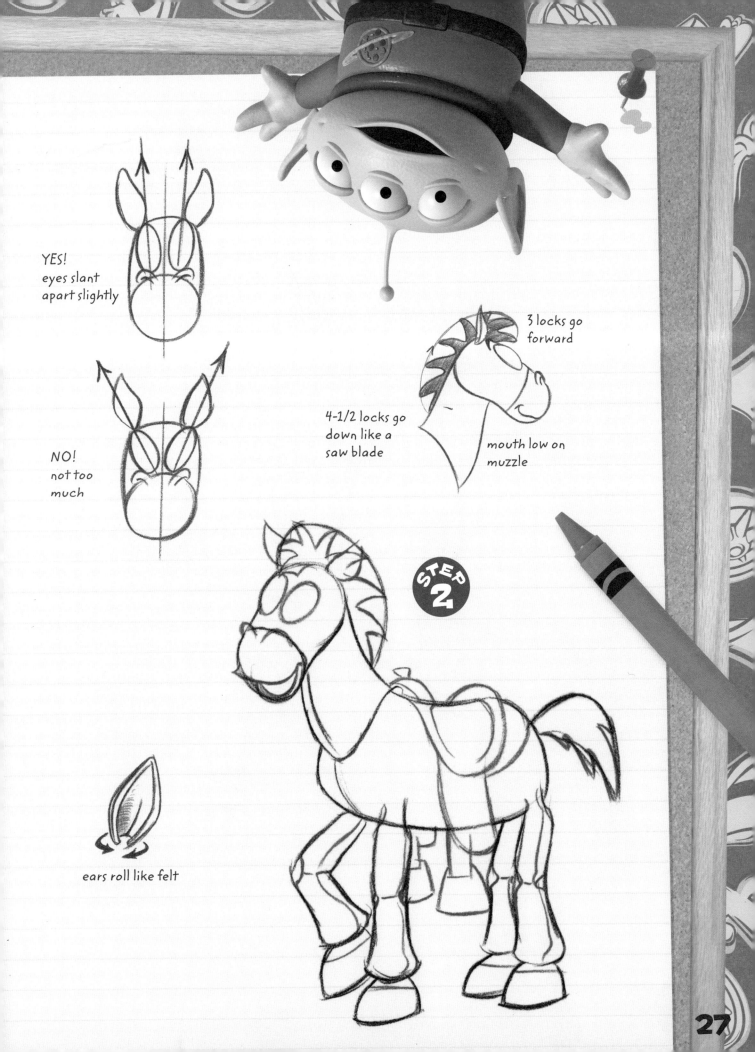

YES!
eyes slant
apart slightly

NO!
not too
much

3 locks go
forward

4-1/2 locks go
down like a
saw blade

mouth low on
muzzle

ears roll like felt

STEP 2

BULLSEYE

STEP 3

bottom points of tail line up

legs are loose and floppy

try to keep a clear line of action

bottom of hoof
is shaped like an
upside-down U

legs are 2
stuffed sections,
almost shaped
like peanuts

This toy dinosaur is one nervous Rex. When he's not worried about being replaced by a bigger dino toy, he's trying to avoid conflict in Andy's room. Rex's growl "almost" scares the other toys.

tail tapers to a point

STEP 1

side of foot

diamond-shaped toenails have a center line

back of foot

keep equal distance between toenails

"yikes!"

"ooooh!"

"aahhh!"

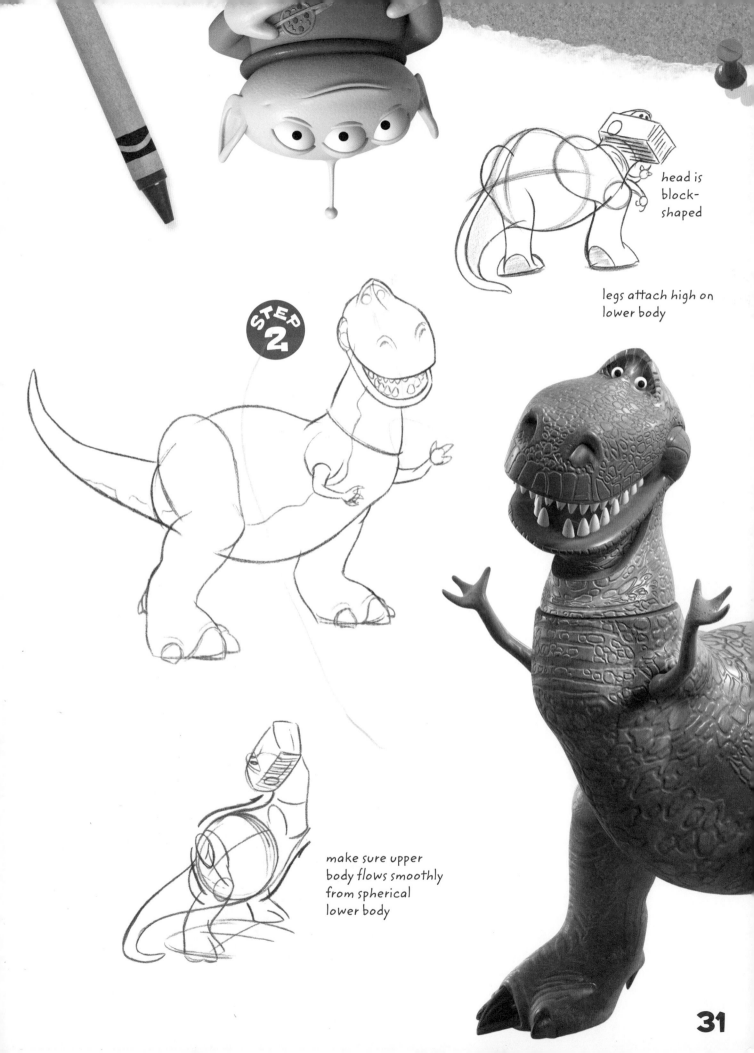

head is block-shaped

legs attach high on lower body

STEP 2

make sure upper body flows smoothly from spherical lower body

31

REX

Rex's pupils
are tiny

basic eye expression

"hmmm."

"what did I step in?"

"the sky is falling!"

cone-shaped teeth

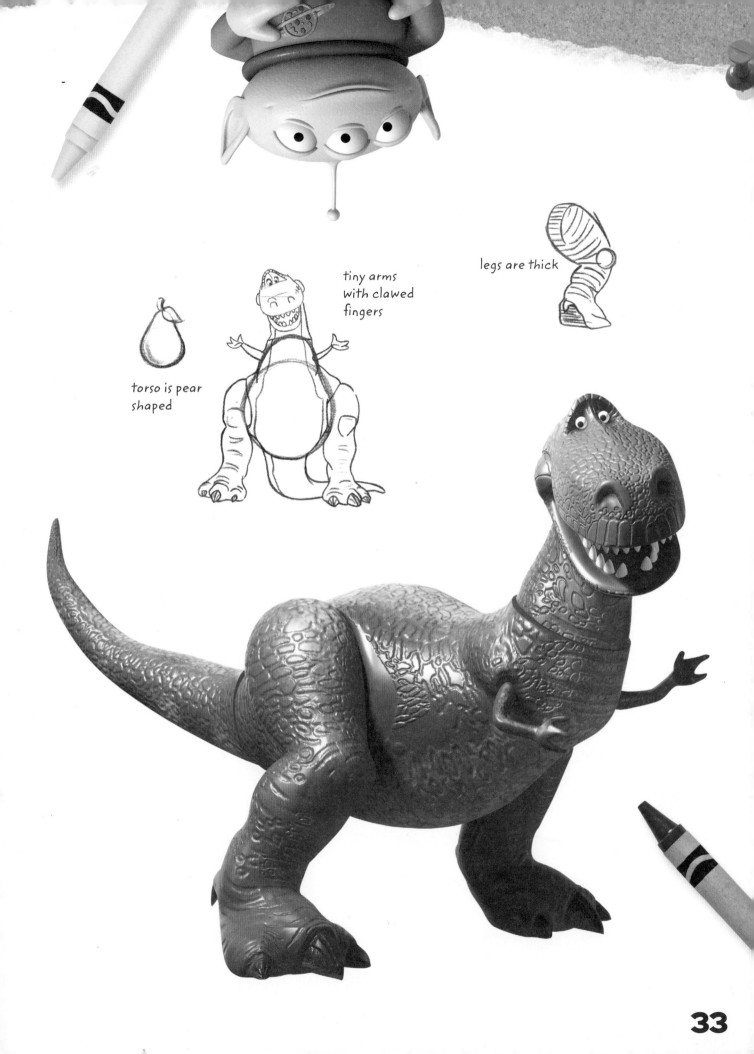

tiny arms
with clawed
fingers

legs are thick

torso is pear
shaped

33

MR. POTATO HEAD

Mr. Potato Head can be cranky sometimes, but he's always there when Mrs. Potato Head needs another spud to lean on.

STEP 1

large oval-shaped eyes

STEP 2

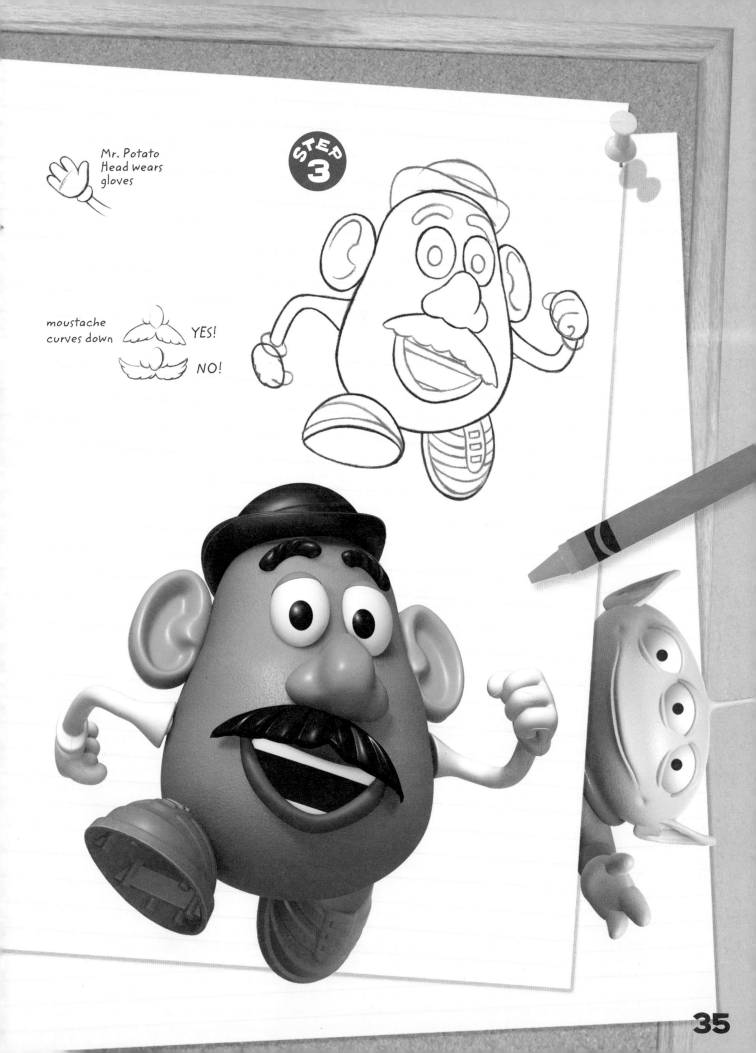

Mr. Potato Head wears gloves

moustache curves down

YES!

NO!

STEP 3

HAMM

You can always count on Hamm to put in his two cents on any topic. As Andy's piggy bank and Mr. Potato Head's buddy (spuddy?), Hamm says what he thinks... especially when he thinks Woody's headed for trouble.

STEP 1

small ears

don't forget his tail and cork!

STEP 2

pear-shaped body

3 toes

eyes can squash and stretch depending on expression

- eyes are high on head
- nostrils lie on top of halfway line on nose
- small bottom teeth

mouth is a small slit on bottom of snout

nose fits on head like a cup on a sphere

STEP 3

Hamm's coin slot

Jessie

Jessie knows what it means to be a toy. She once belonged to a little girl who loved her as much as Andy loves Woody. But that little girl gave Jessie away and in *Toy Story 2*, the brokenhearted cowgirl decided that being a collectible is better than being with a child who might outgrow you. Woody has to remind Jessie what being a toy is all about. In *Toy Story 3*, Jessie feels the same anxiety about being abandoned by her owner—but this time, it leads the whole gang to danger!

STEP 1

YES! she has a button nose

NO!

3 fringe pieces

stitching wraps around cuff

shirt and gauntlet pattern

don't forget
her ponytail

Woody's hat is
triangular

Jessie's hat is
rounder

STEP 2

her hat usually
sits on the back
of her head

STEP 3

Jessie's body is
flexible like a
rag doll's

THE PROSPECTOR

The Prospector may seem like a nice grandfatherly type of fellow at first, but when his true feelings are revealed, it becomes clear that he's just plain selfish and mean. Having never belonged to a child, the Prospector simply doesn't know how to play—or be loved.

STEP 1

head is bell-shaped

moustache changes with mood

beard, brows, and moustache are loose and bushy

STEP 2

relaxed gesture

stretch

body like a half-filled flour sack

excited gesture

squish

The Prospector is never without his pickaxe

boot flares at top

hat curls up in front and back

pointy beard in side view

button detail

small hands with slender fingers

tight-fitting sleeves

SLINKY

"Slink" always has a spring in his step. He's a happy-go-lucky toy dog and one of Woody's strongest supporters. When Woody needs help, Slinky Dog goes the extra mile—or at least as far as his spring will stretch.

STEP 1

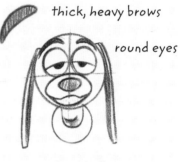

thick, heavy brows

round eyes

head is a ball

STEP 2

back legs have bendable knees

Slinky is a pull toy, so he has a wheel on each foot

body is 2 halves of a sphere attached with a spring

eye lies halfway up on head circle

spring compresses and shortens body

ALIENS

It's a small world for the Alien toys at Pizza Planet. They live to see whom "the Claw" will pluck from their crane-game world. While trapped inside the crane game, the Aliens obey the Claw's calling, but once they leave, they happily switch their loyalty to others—like Mr. Potato Head, much to his chagrin.

STEP 1

STEP 2

STEP 3

GREEN ARMY MEN

Led by Sarge, these soldiers are always ready for a Code Red. Whether they're parachuting from the second floor or running from a toy ball, the Green Army Men move with military precision—even though their feet are attached to solid bases.

STEP 1

STEP 2

STEP 3

ZURG

The Universe—and Al's Toy Barn—is not a safe place with the evil Emperor Zurg on the loose. Zurg is smart enough to escape from the store and strong enough to take on Buzz and New Buzz, but he's unlucky enough to be on the receiving end of Rex's swinging tail.

hands are composed of sharp steel parts with claw-like fingers

fingers resemble armor plates

5 torso rings

STEP 1

angle of horns is about 45 degrees

YES!

NO!

NO!

concave — Zurg's gauntlet

convex — Buzz's gauntlet

"Feet" are 3 wheels

visor appears triangular in all views

8 glowing yellow teeth

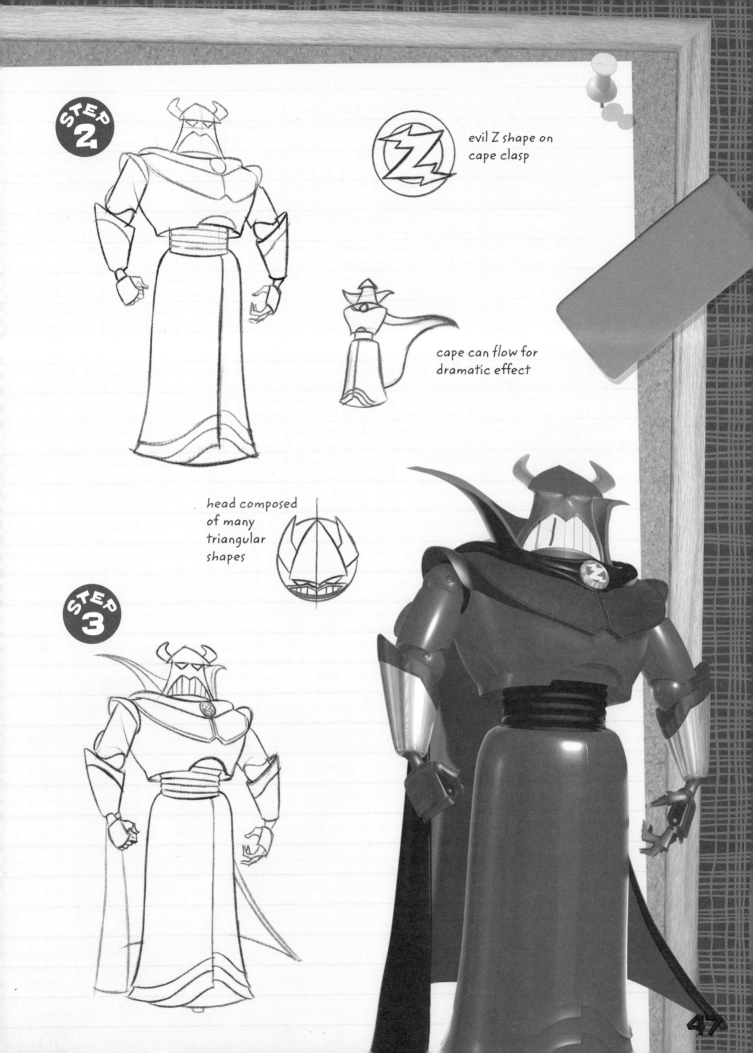

STEP 2

evil Z shape on cape clasp

cape can flow for dramatic effect

head composed of many triangular shapes

STEP 3

47

Bo Peep

When Bo Peep isn't minding her sheep, she's got her eye on Woody. Although "Bo" is part of baby Molly's lamp, she definitely is not a preschool toy. Bo Peep is wise, and she believes in Woody no matter what happens.

STEP 2

STEP 1

3 curls on the back of her head

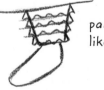

pantaloons look like shingles

48

basic wedge
shape of hat

add curves
and details

NO! neck
too short

YES! keep
neck long

eyes come
halfway
down head

upside-down
triangle mouth

start profile
with a circle

wedge-
shaped
nose

STEP
3

dress looks
like a parasol

LOTSO

In *Toy Story 3*, Lots-o'-Huggin' Bear—a.k.a Lotso—seems like nothing more than the nicest teddy bear at Sunnyside Daycare. But Lotso's true colors are exposed when he traps Andy's toys in the Caterpillar Room with all of the rambunctious toddlers—and later when he leaves the toys to be incinerated at the garbage dump.

STEP 1

eyebrows are wide and bushy

YES!

NO!

ears are 2 half circles

nose is an upside-down rounded triangle

teardrop-shaped paws

STEP 2

3

STEP 3

I'M A HUGGER

eyes are round and set close together

His cane is a wooden mallet

BIG BABY

In *Toy Story 3*, Big Baby (along with Lotso and Chuckles) was accidentally left at a rest stop by his first owner, Daisy. Although Big Baby initially does Lotso's dirty work at Sunnyside Daycare, once he realizes how much he misses his mama, he helps the toys escape from Lotso's grasp.

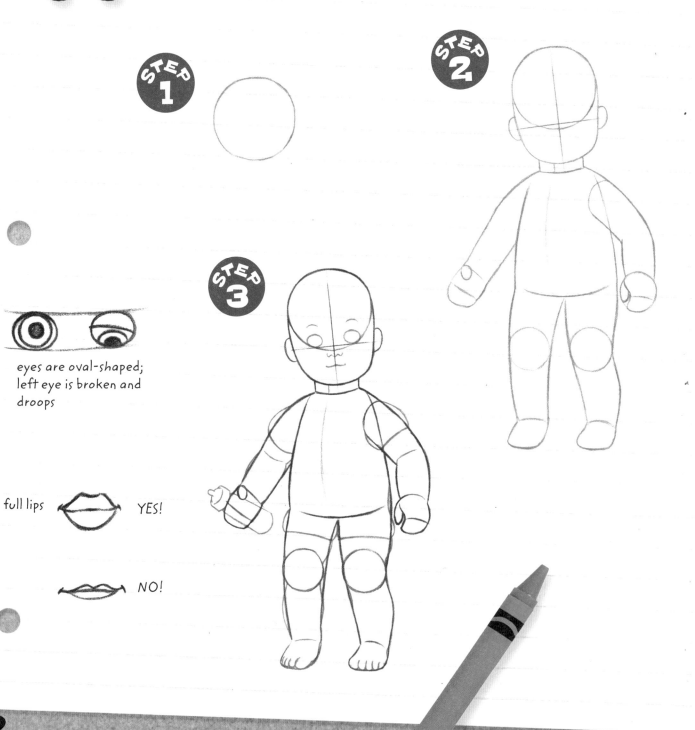

eyes are oval-shaped; left eye is broken and droops

full lips — YES!

NO!

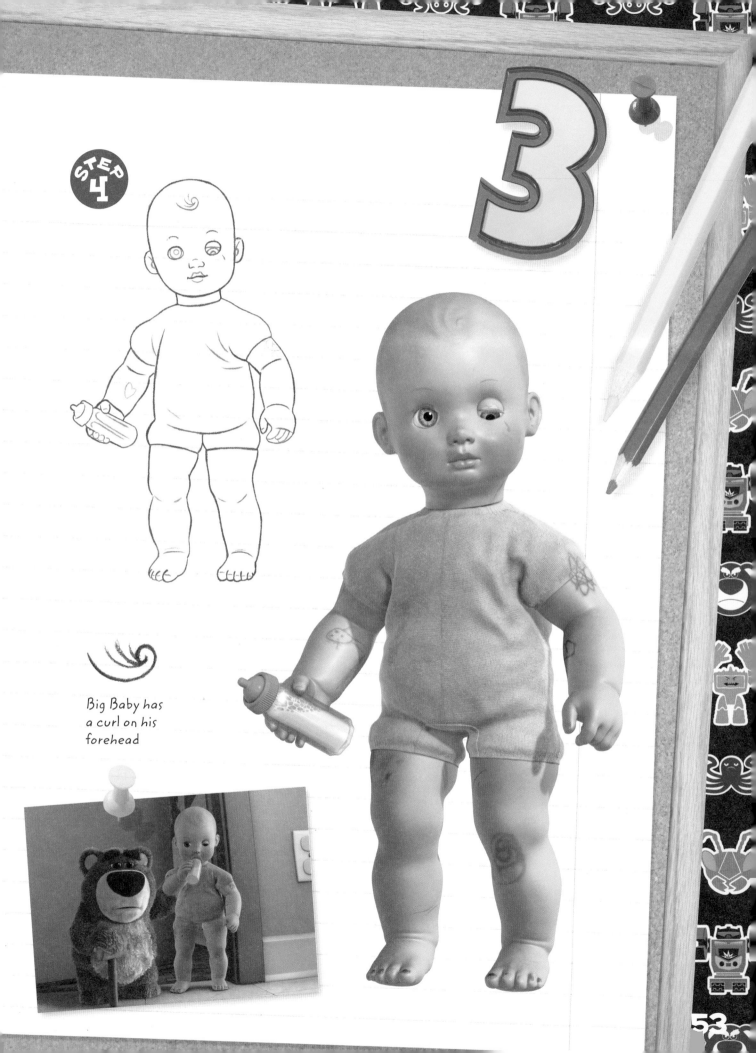

STEP 4

3

Big Baby has a curl on his forehead

CHUNK

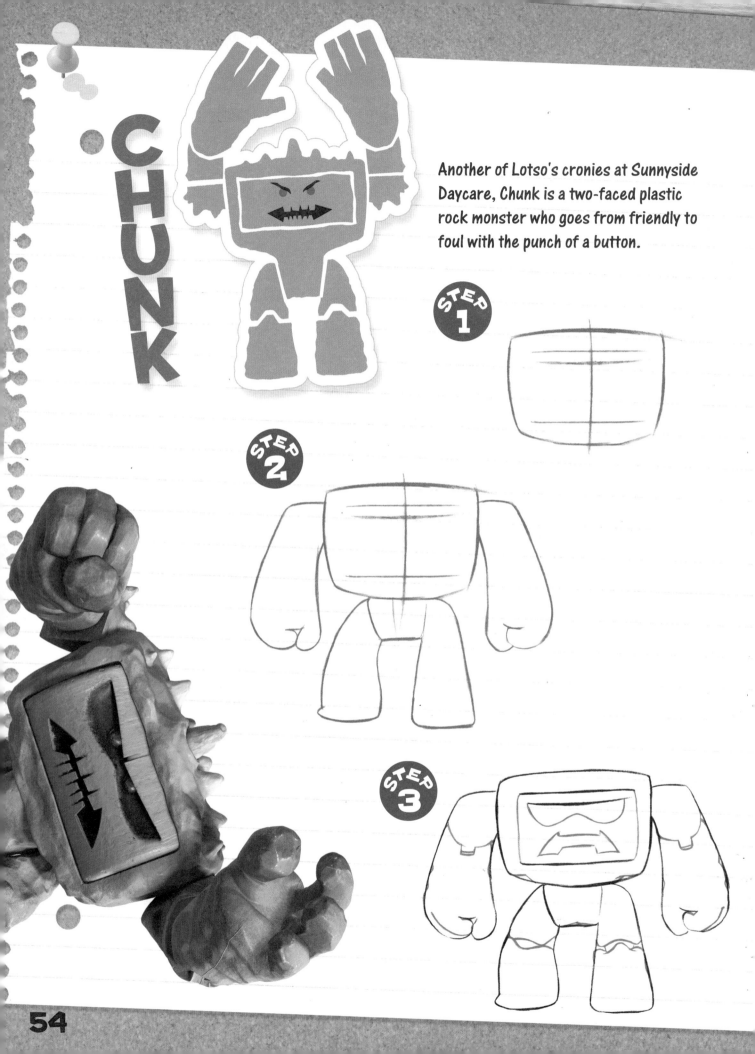

Another of Lotso's cronies at Sunnyside Daycare, Chunk is a two-faced plastic rock monster who goes from friendly to foul with the punch of a button.

STEP 1

STEP 2

STEP 3

STEP 4

Chunk has two faces

MR. PRICKLEPANTS

Mr. Pricklepants is no ordinary hedgehog. This lederhosen-wearing toy is both dramatic and intellectual. He is also very kind to all of the other toys in Bonnie's toy collection.

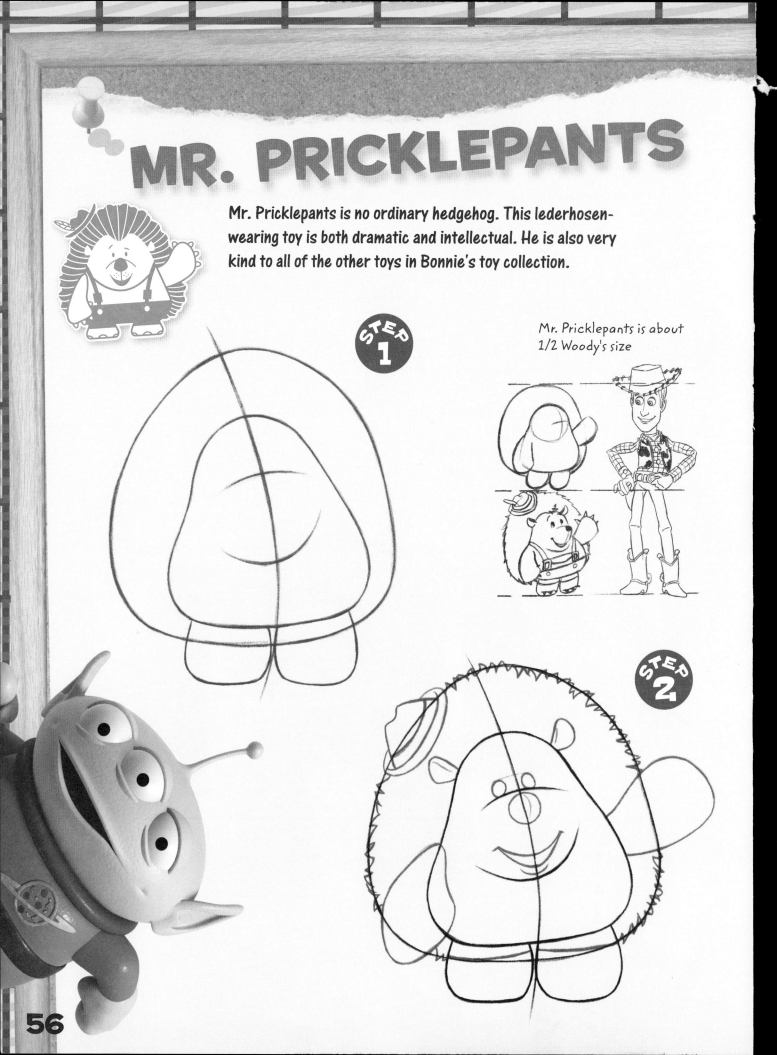

STEP 1

Mr. Pricklepants is about 1/2 Woody's size

STEP 2

body looks like a pear

hat looks like an
upside-down cup
on a saucer

STEP
3

claws
are small
triangles

arms taper

suspenders
have a
buckle

BUTTERCUP

In *Toy Story 3*, Buttercup may look like a cute and cuddly unicorn, but he's really a gruff, no-nonsense member of Bonnie's toy collection.

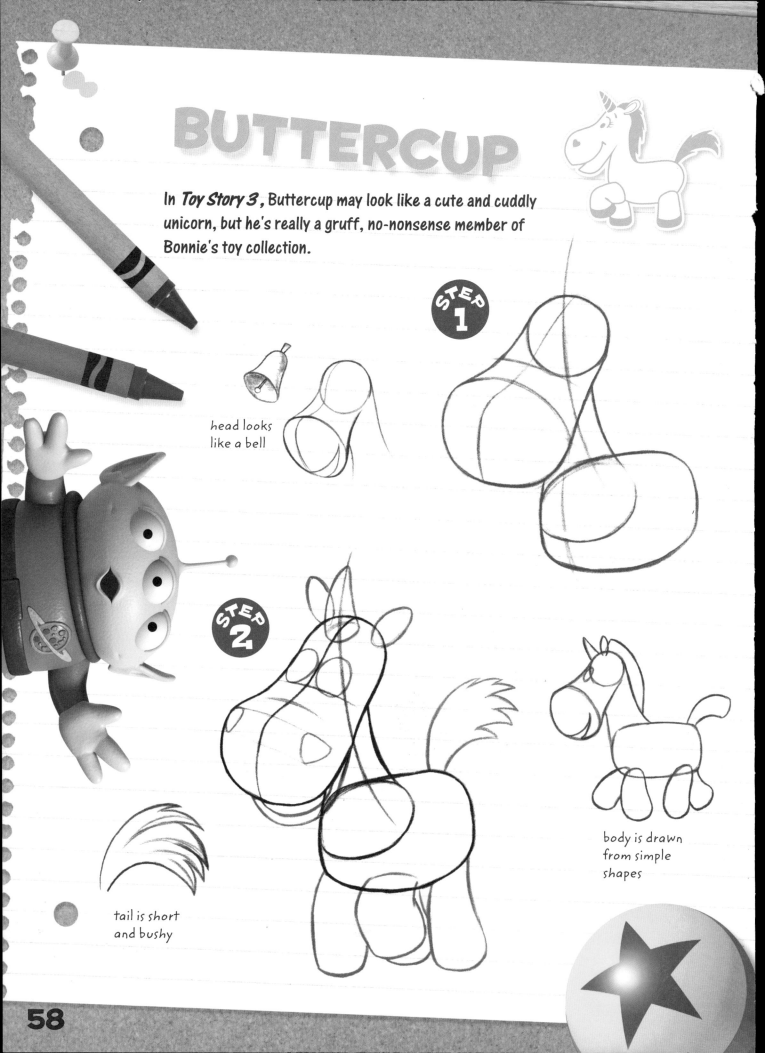

head looks like a bell

STEP 1

STEP 2

tail is short and bushy

body is drawn from simple shapes

horn has 5 parts

nostrils
are heart-
shaped

eyes are ovals,
pupils and irises
are round, and
his eyebrows
follow the
shape of eye

TWITCH

Twitch is the tough, muscular, staff-wielding, insect-headed member of Lotso's gang at Sunnyside Daycare. He doesn't say much, but he's not a bug any of Andy's toys want to mess with.

STEP 1

STEP 2

STEP 3

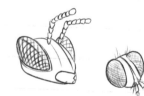

head is triangular and looks like a fly's head

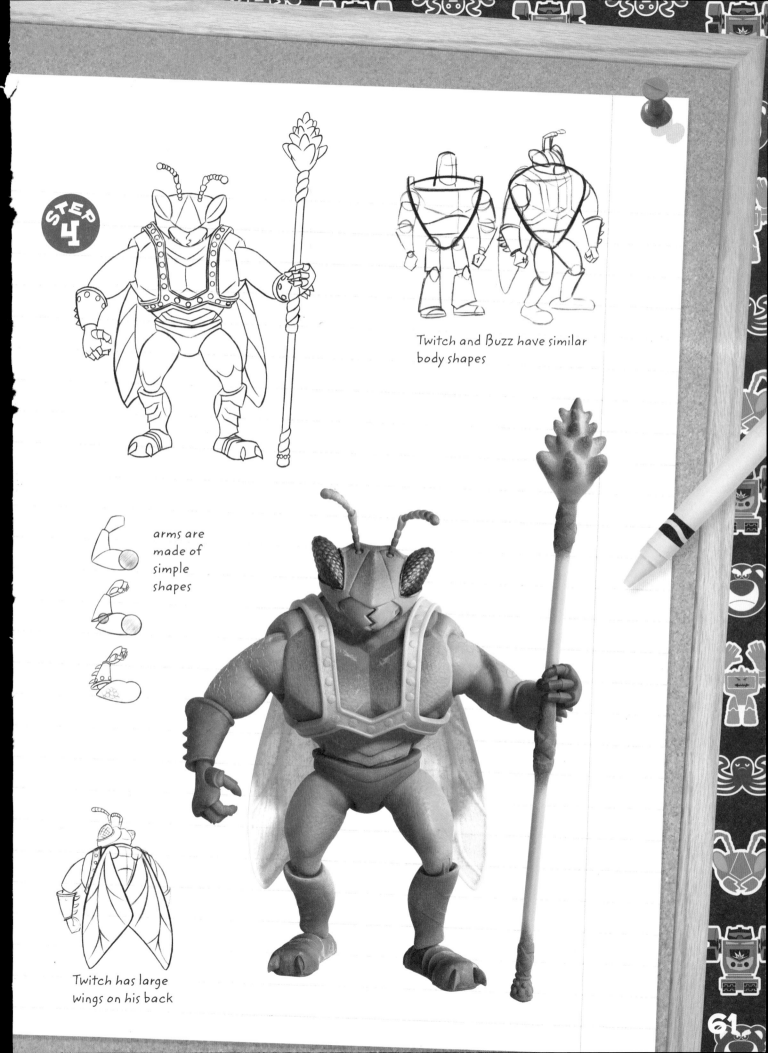

STEP 4

Twitch and Buzz have similar body shapes

arms are made of simple shapes

Twitch has large wings on his back

61

STRETCH

Stretch is a fun-loving glittery-purple octopus with a tough rubber exterior that can withstand even the most extreme rough-and-tumble play at Sunnyside Daycare Center.

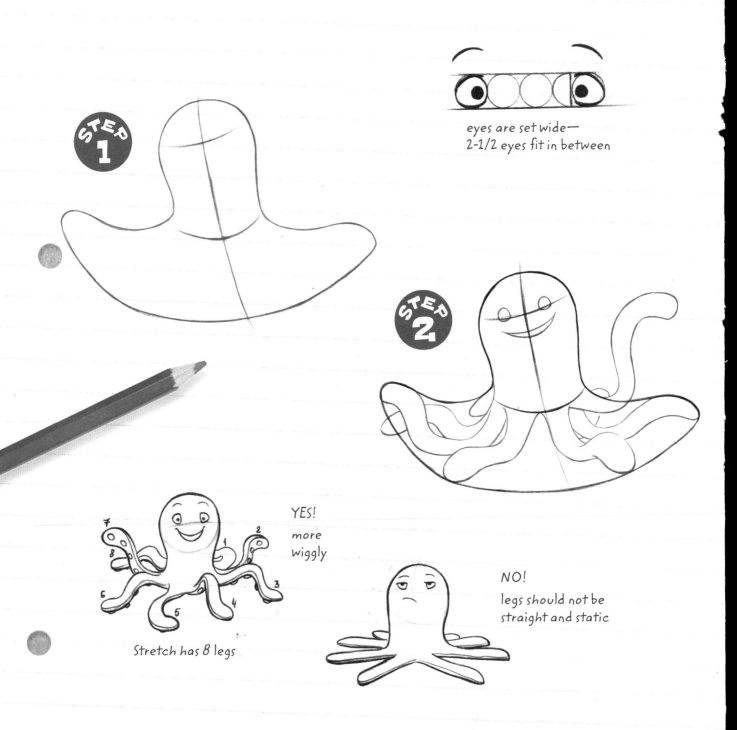

eyes are set wide—
2-1/2 eyes fit in between

STEP 1

STEP 2

YES!
more
wiggly

NO!
legs should not be
straight and static

Stretch has 8 legs

STEP 3

suction cups fit on each leg

legs are pliable and can twist

STEP 4

THE END
Now that you've learned all the tricks to drawing your favorite toys, it's time to have fun! So go ahead—pick up your pencils and draw!